Keto Desserts:

30 Low Carb / High Fat Recipes

Annie DePasquale, MD

FREE BONUS

As a small token of appreciation for purchasing this book,
Dr. Annie would like to offer you a free copy of her next health-
related e-book.

You can get your free gift by clicking here:

http://www.FamilyDocAnnie.com/keto

Disclaimer

The information in this book is for informational purposes only, and is not intended to serve as a substitute for the medical treatment of a qualified physician or healthcare provider.

Acknowledgements

This book is dedicated to all people who have to committed to the keto diet. It may be tough at times, but it will make you healthier and stronger in the end.

Introduction

Hi, I'm Annie DePasquale, a family medicine physician in Washington, D.C., who is extremely passionate about helping my patients with certain dietary preferences.

As someone with a sweet tooth, I know that it can be particularly challenging to find a dessert that is low in carbohydrates. Hopefully this book will provide some recipes to safely satisfy your dessert cravings.

Sincerely,

Dr. Annie

TABLE OF CONTENTS

APPLE CINNAMON CHEESECAKE

This delicious no-bake cheesecake will make your mouth water after just a single bite.

Prep time: 10 minutes

Cook time: 15 minutes

Serves:1

450Cal/ 10g Protein/42g Fat/ 7g Carbs

INGREDIENTS

½ cup sliced apples

3 oz. Cream cheese

¼ cup stevia sweetener

1 tbsp. Butter

2 tbsp. heavy whipping cream

1 tsp. Cinnamon

DIRECTIONS

In a large non-stick skillet, cook the apples in the butter for 10 minutes or until they are soft and tender. In a stand mixer, whip all the remaining ingredients together well. Place the whipped cream cheese in the bottom of a cup and place the apples on top. Serve and enjoy!

APPLE CINNAMON COBBLER

This quick and easy rendition of a classic dessert goes perfectly with a scoop of keto ice cream on top.

Prep time: 10 minutes

Cook time: 30 minutes

Serves: 8

107Cal/ 1g Protein/ 9g Fat/ 7g Carbs

INGREDIENTS

4 cups apples, peeled and sliced

1 tbsp. ground cinnamon + 2 tbsp. stevia sweetener

2 tbsp. vegetable oil

1 cup almond flour

½ cup unsalted butter, softened

¼ cup stevia sweetener

4 tbsp. water

DIRECTIONS

In a non-stick skillet, cook the apples in the vegetable oil over high heat until the apples become soft and tender. Add the cinnamon and 2 tbsp. stevia sweetener to the apples and cook for 1 minute then remove from the heat. Spray a 9x13 baking dish with cooking release spray and fill with the apples. In a large bowl mix all remaining ingredients together well. Place the crumbly batter on top of the blueberries making sure to get them all covered. Place in the oven at 350 degrees for 20 minutes. Allow the cobbler to cool down for 5 minutes before serving. Cut, serve and enjoy!

BANANA LIGHT PUDDING

Here is a great recipe for a quick and easy banana pudding. If you feel the flavor is too light, then you can add some banana extract to boost the flavor.

Prep time: 20 minutes

Cook time: 0 minutes

Serves:10

377Cal/ 6g Protein/32g Fat/ 8g Carbs

INGREDIENTS

½ cup heavy whipping cream

¼ cup stevia

¼ cup banana, mashed

1 tsp. Vanilla extract

DIRECTIONS

Place the heavy cream and stevia in a stand mixer and whip until the cream becomes stiff with peaks. Add the banana and vanilla extract and mix well. Place the pudding in cups or glasses. Refrigerate for at least 1 hour before serving to allow the pudding to set up.

BLUEBERRY ALMOND TRIFLE

A trifle is sort of like a parfait, which is a little bit heavier on the fat content. Trifle usually has a pudding with it, but in this case, we used a mascarpone whip instead.

Prep time: 10 minutes

Cook time: 0 minutes

Serves:1

438Cal/ 7g Protein/44g Fat/ 5g Carbs

INGREDIENTS

¼ cup cream cheese

½ cup blueberries

2 tbsp. heavy whipping cream

2 tbsp. sliced almonds

½ cup mascarpone cheese

¼ cup stevia sweetener

1 tsp. vanilla extract

DIRECIONS

In a stand-up mixer, whip together all of the ingredients except for the blueberries and almonds. Then use a bowl or cup to layer the mixture with the berries and almonds, alternating layers until the ingredients are used up to create a trifle. Refrigerate for at least 1 hour before serving. Enjoy!

BLUEBERRY COBBLER

Here is a quick and easy version of a classic dessert. You can use either fresh or frozen blueberries for this awesome low carb dessert!

Prep time: 10 minutes

Cook time: 30 minutes

Serves: 8

103Cal/ 1g Protein/ 8g Fat/ 7g Carbs

INGREDIENTS

3 cups blueberries

1 cup almond flour

½ cup butter, softened

¼ cup stcvia sweetener

4 tbsp. water

DIRECTIONS

Spray a 9x13 baking dish with cooking release spray and fill with the blueberries. In a large bowl mix all remaining ingredients together well. The mixture should be a crumbled and not smooth. Place the crumbly batter on top of the blueberries making sure to get them all covered. Place in the oven at 325 degrees for 30 minutes. Allow the cobbler to cool down for 5 minutes before serving. Cut, serve and enjoy!

BROOKIES

This dessert is the unique combination of a brownie and a cookie. This version is an easy 'no bake' recipe.

Prep time: 1 hour 20 minutes

Cook time: 0 minutes

Serves: 20

97Cal/ 5g Protein/ 8g Fat/ 5g Carbs

INGREDIENTS

2 cups Nutella spread

¼ cup maple syrup

¾ cup almond flour

¼ cup ketogenic chocolate chips

DIRECTIONS

Place Nutella and maple syrup in a large microwaveable safe bowl and melt for about 1 minute. Mix well then add the flour and chocolate chips. Mix everything together well until a doughy batter is formed. Take small scoops of batter and form into cookie shapes and place on a greased cookie sheet or plate. Refrigerate for at least 1 hour before serving the cut and enjoy!

CHERRY LIMEADE PIE

Do you enjoy an ice cold, refreshing cherry limeade on a hot summer day? Well, if you do, this dessert is right up your alley!

Prep time: 10 minutes

Cook time: 2 hours 10 minutes

Serves: 8

201Cal/ 5g Protein/ 16g Fat/ 8g Carbs

INGREDIENTS

1 ½ cups maraschino cherries

Zest and juice of 2 limes

1 cup plain Greek yogurt

1 cup almond flour

¼ cup unsalted butter (room temperature)

½ tsp. salt

3 tbsp. ice water

DIRECTIONS

For the pie crust dough:

In a stand-up mixer, mix flour, salt and butter. Consistency should be crumbly. Add ice water a mix to form a soft dough. Form into a thick disk, wrap in plastic and refrigerate overnight. Dust with flour dough and counter. Roll out dough to fit a 9 ½ inch pie dish. Form the dough on the pan and bake in the oven at 400 for 10 min or until the crust becomes golden brown.

For the pie filling:

In a large bowl, mix the lime zest and juice, cherries and yogurt until smooth. Place the mixture in a cooked pie crust. Refrigerate for 2 hours then slice into 8 slices. 8 portions per pie.

CHOCOLATE COVERED COCONUTS

Here is another recipe similar to a Mound's candy bar, but it has a texture more like a cake ball.

Prep time: 50 minutes

Cook time: 0 minutes

Serves: 18

40Cal/ 1g Protein/ 4g Fat/ 3g Carbs

INGREDIENTS

½ cup almond flour

¼ cup maple syrup

4 tbsp. coconut cream

1 cup of ketogenic chocolate chips

1 ½ cups unsweetened, shredded coconut

DIRECTIONS

Place the coconut, coconut cream, maple syrup and flour into a bowl or standing mixer and whisk everything together until a batter forms. Using a small melon baller or spoon, scoop out small portions of the coconut batter and form them into small 1" balls. Place the balls in the freezer for 30 minutes. Melt the chocolate over a double boiler (pot of boiling water with a metal bowl on top). Carefully roll the coconut balls in the chocolate until they are completely covered them place them on a greased sheet pan or plate. Place them in the fridge for about 20 minutes. Serve and enjoy!

CHOCOLATE CREAM PIE

Ever wish you could have a slice of chocolate meringue pie and not feel completely guilty about all the carbs you are eating? Well, now you can with this wonderful low carb dessert.

Prep time: 10 minutes

Cook time: 2 hours 10 minutes

Serves: 8

252Cal/ 6g Protein/ 23g Fat/ 10g Carbs

INGREDIENTS

¼ cup cream cheese

¼ cup ketogenic chocolate chips

¼ cup stevia sweetener

¼ cup heavy whipping cream

1 tsp. vanilla extract

1 cup plain Greek yogurt

1 cup almond flour

¼ cup unsalted butter (room temperature)

½ tsp. salt

3 tbsp. ice water

DIRECTIONS

For the pie crust:

In a stand-up mixer, mix flour, salt and butter. Consistency should be crumbly. Add ice water a mix to form a soft dough. Form into a thick disk, wrap in plastic and refrigerate overnight. Dust with flour dough and counter. Roll out dough to fit a 9 ½ inch pie dish. Form the dough on the pan and bake in the oven at 400 for 10 min or until the crust becomes golden brown.

For the pie filling:

Melt the chocolate chips in a microwave or double boiler.
Using a stand mixer, whip all the remaining
ingredients together until everything is smooth. Place mixture in cooked pie crust.
Refrigerate for 2 hours then slice into 8 slices. 8 portions per pie.

CHOCOLATE CRÈME DE MINTH

The only thing this crème brulee is missing from the traditional recipe is the caramelized sugar coating, but you won't miss it with the delicious taste of this silky pudding.

Prep time: 10 minutes

Cook time: 30 minutes

Serves:1

337Cal/ 8g Protein/342g Fat/ 4g Carbs

INGREDIENTS

½ cup heavy whipping cream

¼ cup milk

2 egg yolks

¼ cup stevia

2 tbsp. ketogenic chocolate chips

1 tbsp. fresh mint leaves, chopped

1 tsp. mint extract

DIRECTIONS

In a saucepot, heat the cream, milk, mint extract and leaves to a low simmer. In a bowl, add the eggs and stevia and whisk well. Temper the milk with the egg mixture by adding a little bit of the heated milk to the egg mixture while stirring. Do this until everything is combined fully. Strain the mixture back into the saucepot to remove the mint leaves and continue to cook over a low simmer for 2 minutes then remove from the heat. Place the mixture in an oven safe baking dish and sprinkle in the chocolate chips. Place in the oven at 300 degrees for 15 minutes. Remove from the oven and place in the fridge. Allow to cool down completely or for at least 1 hour before serving.

CHOCOLATE MOUSSE

This chocolate mousse is very similar to a chocolate pudding, however the texture and flavors are much lighter to create a less heavy dessert!

Prep time: 10 minutes

Cook time: 0 minutes

Serves:1

311Cal/ 7g Protein/37g Fat/ 6g Carbs

INGREDIENTS

¼ cup cream cheese

¼ cup ketogenic chocolate chips

¼ cup stevia sweetener

¼ cup heavy whipping cream

1 tsp. vanilla extract

DIRECTIONS

Melt the chocolate chips in a microwave or double boiler. Using a stand mixer, whip all the ingredients together until everything is smooth. Place the chocolate mousse into jars or cups, serve and enjoy! You may garnish with a little cocoa powder if you like.

CHOCOLATE PEANUT CAKE POPS

This recipe is a fun and deliciously indulgent truffle on a stick!

Prep time: 20 minutes

Cook time: 0 minutes

Serves:10

103Cal/ 5g Protein/8g Fat/ 4g Carbs

INGREDIENTS

¾ cup almond flour

2 cups Nutella

½ cup crushed peanuts

¼ cup maple syrup

DIRECTIONS

In a food processor, blend all of the ingredients, except the peanuts, together well till a paste is formed. Use a melon baller to scoop out small portions and roll them into balls. Place the balls on a greased sheet tray or plate and stick a lollipop stick in the center standing straight up. Then roll and press the peanuts onto the cake pops till fully coated. Place the cake pops in the fridge for at least 30 minutes before serving.

CHOCOLATE TRUFFLES

This is a classic dessert found commonly in French bakeries. This rich and usually bite size treat is sure to brighten your day!

Prep time: 50 minutes

Cook time: 0 minutes

Serves: 6

63Cal/ 1g Protein/ 5g Fat/ 7g Carbs

INGREDIENTS

4 oz. ketogenic chocolate chips

¼ cup heavy whipping cream

1 tsp. vanilla extract

DIRECTIONS

Melt the chocolate over a double boiler (pot of boiling water with a metal bowl on top). Then add the cream and vanilla extract to the chocolate and whisk well. Spray a pan with cooking release spray and pour the chocolate mixture into the pan. Refrigerate for at least 1 hour or until the chocolate has become firm. Using a small melon baller or spoon, scoop out small portions and form into balls. Serve and enjoy!

COCONUT CRANBERRY LOLLIPOPS

Here is another delicious and refreshing truffle on a stick!

Prep time: 50 minutes

Cook time: 0 minutes

Serves: 10

134Cal/ 3g Protein/11g Fat/ 5g Carbs

INGREDIENTS

1 ½ cups shredded unsweetened coconut

¼ cup dried cranberries

2 tbsp. stevia sweetener

1 tbsp. coconut oil

4 tbsp. almond milk

1 cup ketogenic chocolate chips

DIRECTIONS

In a food processor, blend all of the ingredients together well till a paste is formed. Use a melon baller to scoop out small portions and roll them into balls. Place the balls on a greased sheet tray or plate and stick a lollipop stick in the center standing straight up. Place the balls in the freezer for 1 hour. Melt the chocolate in the microwave or over a double boiler. Once frozen, dip the lollipops into the chocolate to coat them completely then transfer back to the place. Place the lollipops in the fridge for at least 30 minutes before serving.

COCONUT KRISPY TREATS

This dessert is made in the same way Rice Krispy treats are made. They are very easy to make, low in carbs, and full of delicious flavor!

Prep time: 1 hour 10 minutes

Cook time: 0 minutes

Serves: 15

108Cal/ 2g Protein/ 11g Fat/ 3g Carbs

INGREDIENTS

3 cups shredded unsweetened coconut

¼ cup maple syrup

¾ cup coconut oil

DIRECTIONS

Spray a baking dish with cooking spray. In a large bowl or stand mixer, mix all ingredients together well until the batter is lumpy. Place the batter in the greased baking pan and press down with a spoon to spread out evenly. Refrigerate for at least 1 hour then cut and serve!

ELVIS LOLLIPOPS

Elvis always enjoyed his signature sandwich -- a peanut butter and banana sandwich. Here is a wonderful rendition of that sandwich made into a small treat.

Prep time: 50 minutes

Cook time: 0 minutes

Serves: 10

140Cal/ 5g Protein/ 8g Fat/ 9g Carbs

INGREDIENTS

½ cup creamy peanut butter

¼ cup almond flour

2 tbsp. Maple syrup

1 banana, cut into ½" thick slices

DIRECTIONS

Place all of the ingredients, except for the bananas, into a bowl or standing mixer and whisk everything together until a batter forms. Using a small melon baller or spoon, scoop out small portions of the peanut butter batter and form them into small 1" balls around the banana slices. Place a lollipop stick in the center of the battered ball sticking straight up. Place the balls in the fridge for 30 minutes before serving. Serve and enjoy!

FLOURLESS CHOCOLATE CAKE

This is an indulgent, classic dessert, which also happens to be gluten free.

Prep time: 15 minutes

Cook time: 25 minutes

Serves: 10

151Cal/ 6g Protein/ 14g Fat/ 9g Carbs

INGREDIENTS

8 oz. ketogenic chocolate chips

8 oz. unsalted butter

1 cup stevia sweetener

6 large eggs

1 cup cocoa powder

DIRECTIONS

Boil a large pot of water. Place a metal bowl on top of the pot sealing it off, this is called a double boiler. Place the dark chocolate and butter in the bowl and mix with a spatula until the chocolate and butter have melted together. Remove from the heat and whisk in the stevia sweetener. Then add the eggs and whisk well. Carefully fold in the cocoa powder until everything is fully incorporated. Spray an 8x8 baking pan with cooking spray and fill up with batter. Bake in the oven at 375 degrees for 25 minutes. Remove from the oven and allow to cool before serving.

FRUITY PEBBLES BRULEE

This is a fun twist on a classic crème brulee.

Prep time: 10 minutes

Cook time: 30 minutes

Serves:1

311Cal/ 7g Protein/30g Fat/ 8g Carbs

INGREDIENTS

½ cup heavy whipping cream

1 cup fruity pebbles

¼ cup milk

2 egg yolks

2 tbsp. stevia sweetener

DIRECTIONS

Place the milk, heavy cream and fruity pebbles in a bowl together and allow to sit for 20 minutes. Strain the milk mixture to remove the fruity pebbles. In a saucepot, heat the cream mixture to a low simmer. In a bowl, add the eggs and stevia and whisk well. Temper the milk with the egg mixture by adding a little bit of the heated milk to the egg mixture while stirring. Do this until everything is combined fully. Continue to cook over a low simmer for 2 minutes then remove from the heat. Place the mixture in an oven safe baking dish and place in the oven at 300 degrees for 15 minutes. Remove from the oven and place in the fridge. Allow to cool down completely or for at least 1 hour before serving.

KETO MOUNDS BARS

This dessert tastes just like a Mounds candy bar, but is super low in carbs!

Prep time: 1 hour 20 minutes

Cook time: 0 minutes

Serves: 20

111Cal/ 2g Protein/ 11g Fat/ 5g Carbs

INGREDIENTS

3 cups shredded unsweetened coconut

¼ cup maple syrup

½ cup coconut oil

1 cup ketogenic chocolate chips

DIRECTIONS

Place all ingredients in a large bowl except for the chocolate and mix well until the batter is lumpy. Melt the chocolate in the microwave or over a double boiler on the stove. Spray a baking dish with cooking release spray and place the coconut batter in the pan. Use a spoon to smooth out the batter evenly in the pan. Gently pour the melted chocolate over the coconut batter in the pan and spread out evenly. Refrigerate for at least 1 hour before serving the cut and enjoy!

KETO REESE'S BARS

This dessert tastes just like a Reese's peanut butter cup!

Prep time: 20 minutes

Cook time: 0 minutes

Serves: 20

139Cal/ 8g Protein/ 10g Fat/ 5g Carbs

INGREDIENTS

2 cups creamy peanut butter

¼ cup maple syrup

¾ cup almond flour

1 cup ketogenic chocolate chips

DIRECTIONS

Place peanut butter and maple syrup in a large microwaveable safe bowl and melt for about 1 minute. Mix well then add the flour. Mix everything together well until a doughy batter is formed. Spray a baking dish with cooking release spray and pour the peanut butter batter in the pan and press out evenly with a spoon. Melt the chocolate in the microwave or on a double boiler and pour over the peanut butter batter in the pan. Spread out the chocolate evenly over the batter. Refrigerate for at least 1 hour before serving, cut and enjoy!

KEY LIME MOUSSE

This key lime recipe is very similar in flavor to a key lime pie. The only difference is that there is no crust. What it lacks in crust, it makes up for in flavor!

Prep time: 10 minutes

Cook time: 0 minutes

Serves:1

438Cal/ 7g Protein/44g Fat/ 4g Carbs

INGREDIENTS

Zest and juice of 1 lime

4 oz. light cream cheese

¼ cup stevia sweetener

3 tbsp. heavy whipping cream

DIRECTIONS

Using a stand mixer, whip all the ingredients together until everything is smooth. Place the key lime whip into jars or cups, serve and enjoy!

KIT KAT BARS

This dessert tastes just like a Kit Kat candy bar!

Prep time: 1 hour 10 minutes

Cook time: 0 minutes

Serves: 20

155Cal/ 7g Protein/ 12g Fat/ 4g Carbs

INGREDIENTS

1 ½ cups ketogenic chocolate chips

1 cup almond butter

¼ cup maple syrup

1 cup almonds, crushed

1 cup peanuts, crushed

1 cup cashews, crushed

DIRECTIONS

Place all ingredients in a large microwaveable safe bowl except for the nuts. Microwave for 2-3 minutes and mix until everything is melted and mixed well. Add the nuts and mix well again. Spray a baking dish with cooking release spray. Add the batter to the pan and smooth out evenly with a spoon. Refrigerate for at least 1 hour before serving the cut and enjoy!

MOCHA KAHLUA CHOCOLATES

These small desserts are definitely a guilty pleasure!

Prep time: 50 minutes

Cook time: 10 minutes

Serves: 8

103Cal/ 1g Protein/ 7g Fat/ 9g Carbs

INGREDIENTS

4 oz. ketogenic chocolate chips

¼ cup heavy whipping cream

¼ cup brewed coffee

1 tbsp. Kahlua liqueur

DIRECTIONS

Melt the chocolate over a double boiler (pot of boiling water with a metal bowl on top). Then add the rest of the ingredients and whisk well. Spray a pan with cooking release spray and pour the chocolate mixture into the pan. Refrigerate for at least 1 hour or until the chocolate has become firm. Using a small melon baller or spoon, scoop out small portions and form into balls. Serve and enjoy!

MOLTEN LAVA CAKE

This classic dessert can also be made in the microwave. Just scoop some batter into a coffee cup and zap it for a few minutes, viola!

Prep time: 15 minutes

Cook time: 20 minutes

Serves: 10

151Cal/ 7g Protein/ 15g Fat/ 9g Carbs

INGREDIENTS

8 oz. ketogenic chocolate chips

8 oz. unsalted butter

1 cup stevia sweetener

6 large eggs

1 cup cocoa powder

DIRECTIONS

Boil a large pot of water. Place a metal bowl on top of the pot sealing it off, this is called a double boiler. Place the dark chocolate and butter in the bowl and mix with a spatula until the chocolate and butter have melted together. Remove from the heat and whisk in the stevia sweetener. Then add the eggs and whisk well. Carefully fold in the cocoa powder until everything is fully incorporated. Spray aa muffin tray with cooking spray and fill up with batter ¾ the way up. Bake in the oven at 325 degrees or 20 minutes, or 15 if you want a gooier center. Remove from the oven and allow to cool before serving.

ORANGE VANILLA PANNA COTTA

This recipe for flan is extremely low in calories and carbs!

Prep time: 1 hour

Cook time: 10 minutes

Serves:1

84Cal/ 4g Protein/3g Fat/ 9g Carbs

INGREDIENTS

½ cup milk

2 tbsp. Stevia sweetener

1 cup cold water

1 gelatin sheet

Juice and zest of 1 orange

1 tsp. vanilla extract

½ vanilla bean, scraped

DIRECTIONS

Place the gelatin sheet in a bowl and submerge in the cold water. Using a saucepot, heat the milk to a low simmer. Remove the gelatin sheet from the water and add it to the heated milk. Stir well and add all the remaining ingredients. Remove from the heat and stir well. Pour the mixture into small cups or bowls and place in the fridge. Allow to cool for at least 1 hour so they will set up. Serve and enjoy!

PEACH PECAN PARFAIT

This is delicious parfait is perfect for a hot summer's day. It tastes like a pecan pie mixed with peaches. Yummy!

Prep time: 10 minutes

Cook time: 0 minutes

Serves:1

438Cal/ 6g Protein/44g Fat/ 7g Carbs

INGREDIENTS

¼ cup light cream cheese

¼ cup sliced peaches

2 tbsp. heavy whipping cream

2 tbsp. crushed pecans

1/2 cup mascarpone cheese

¼ cup stevia sweetener

1 tsp. vanilla extract

DIRECTIONS

In a stand mixer, whip together all of the ingredients except for the pecans and peaches. Then use a bowl or cup to layer the mixture with the peaches and pecans to create a parfait. Refrigerate for at least 1 hour before serving. Enjoy!

PEPPERMINT CHOCOLATES

These are perfect to serve around the holiday season. The flavor will surely remind you of Christmas.

Prep time: 50 minutes

Cook time: 0 minutes

Serves: 6

63Cal/ 1g Protein/ 5g Fat/ 7g Carbs

INGREDIENTS

4 oz. Ketogenic chocolate chips

¼ cup heavy whipping cream

2 tbsp. chopped fresh mint

2 tbsp. Peppermint liqueur

1 tsp. crushed candy canes (optional for décor)

DIRECTIONS

Melt the chocolate over a double boiler (pot of boiling water with a metal bowl on top). In a blender, blend the mint and heavy cream together. Strain the cream through a fine mesh colander making sure to get out as much of leaves as possible. Then add the cream and the rest of the ingredients to the chocolate and whisk well. Spray a pan with cooking release spray and pour the chocolate mixture into the pan. Refrigerate for at least 1 hour or until the chocolate has become firm. Using a small melon baller or spoon, scoop out small portions and form into balls. If you want you can sprinkle crushed candy canes on top of the truffles but only a little bit to act as an accent. Serve and enjoy!

SMORE'S TRUFFLES

This winning combo is a mix between a classic campfire smore and a chocolate truffle!

Prep time: 50 minutes

Cook time: 0 minutes

Serves: 6

68Cal/ 1g Protein/ 5g Fat/ 8g Carbs

INGREDIENTS

4 oz. ketogenic chocolate chips

¼ cup heavy whipping cream

10 miniature marshmallows

1 graham cracker, crushed

1 tsp. vanilla extract

DIRECTIONS

Melt the chocolate over a double boiler (pot of boiling water with a metal bowl on top). Then add the cream and vanilla extract to the chocolate and whisk well. Spray a pan with cooking release spray and pour the chocolate mixture into the pan. Refrigerate for at least 1 hour or until the chocolate has become firm. Using a small melon baller or spoon, scoop out small portions. Form the chocolate into balls covering a marshmallow so it is in the middle of the truffle ball. Coat the outside of the truffle in crushed graham crackers. Serve and enjoy! You may also shape this into whatever shape you like, the chocolate will meld well but do not handle it too long otherwise it will melt.

SNICKERS LOLLIPOPS

Who doesn't love a Snicker's bar on a stick?

Prep time: 50 minutes

Cook time: 0 minutes

Serves: 10

89Cal/ 4g Protein/ 7g Fat/ 4g Carbs

INGREDIENTS

1 cup almond flour

¼ cup stevia sweetener

2 tbsp. maple syrup

¼ cup almond milk

¼ cup almond butter

1 cup ketogenic chocolate chips

¼ cup coconut oil

DIRECTIONS

Place all of the ingredients, except for the chocolate, almond butter and coconut oil, into a bowl or standing mixer and whisk everything together until a batter forms. Using a small melon baller or spoon, scoop out small portions of the batter and form them into small 1" balls. Place a lollipop stick in the center of the battered ball sticking straight up. Place the balls in the freezer for 30 minutes. In a small bowl whisk the coconut oil and almond butter together well. Remove the balls from the freezer and coat them in the mixture, then replace them back in the freezer for 30 minutes. Melt the chocolate over a double boiler (pot of boiling water with a metal bowl on top). Carefully roll the balls in the chocolate until they are completely covered then place them on a greased sheet pan or plate. Place them in the fridge for about 20 minutes before serving. Serve and enjoy!

VANILLA BEAN CRÈME BRULEE

This dessert is the crème de la crème!

Prep time: 10 minutes

Cook time: 30 minutes

Serves:1

317Cal/ 7g Protein/332g Fat/ 3g Carbs

INGREDIENTS

½ cup heavy whipping cream

¼ cup milk

2 egg yolks

¼ cup stevia sweetener

1 tsp. vanilla extract

½ vanilla bean, scraped

DIRECTIONS

In a saucepot, heat the cream, milk, vanilla extract and bean to a low simmer. In a bowl, add the eggs and stevia and whisk well. Temper the milk with the egg mixture by adding a little bit of the heated milk to the egg mixture while stirring. Do this until everything is combined fully. Continue to cook over a low simmer for 2 minutes then remove from the heat. place the mixture in an oven safe baking dish and place in the oven at 300 degrees for 15 minutes. Remove from the oven and place in the fridge. Allow to cool down completely or for at least 1 hour before serving.

ABOUT THE AUTHOR

Annie DePasquale MD is an actively practicing family physician and mother of two - soon-to-be three! When not caring for her family or patients, she is helping to spread good family medicine practices through her writing and social media pursuits.

Visit her at http://www.FamilyDocAnnie.com

She is also on Facebook and Twitter. #FamilyDocAnnie

If you enjoyed this book, please leave a quick review on Amazon. This would be tremendously appreciated.

OTHER BOOKS

Dr. Annie DePasquale's other published books Include:

Delectable Diabetes Desserts: 30 Recipes With 10 Carbs or Less

Diabetes & Hypertension Cookbook: 45 Recipes for Low Carb / Low Salt Diet

Gluten Free Desserts: 30 Delicious Recipes

Cooking With Kids: 30 Healthy Recipes Your Kids Will Love To Make

Stress Less: 50 Practical Tips to Decrease Your Daily Stress

Stop Smoking Now

FREE BONUS

As a small token of appreciation for purchasing this book, Dr. Annie would like to offer you a free copy of her next health-related e-book.

You can get your free gift by clicking here:

http://www.FamilyDocAnnie.com/4811

Made in the USA
San Bernardino, CA
27 December 2018